MARTIN LUTHER'S
Christmas Book

MARTIN LUTHER'S
Christmas Book

edited by

ROLAND H. BAINTON

Augsburg

MINNEAPOLIS

MARTIN LUTHER'S CHRISTMAS BOOK

Cover Design by Craig P. Claeys
Text Design by Lois Stanfield, LightSource Images

Library of Congress Cataloging-in-Publication Data

Luther, Martin, 1483–1546.
    [Sermons. English. Selections]
    Martin Luther's Christmas book / edited by Roland H. Bainton.
       p.   cm.
    Excerpts from 30 Christmas sermons.
    Includes bibliographical references.
    ISBN 0-8066-3577-0 (alk. paper)
    1. Lutheran Church—Sermons—Early works to 1800. 2. Christmas sermons—
Early works to 1800. I. Bainton, Roland Herbert, 1894– . II. Title.
BV4257.L88   1997
252 ' .615—dc21
                                         97-28979
                                           CIP

The paper used in this publication meets the minimum requirements of American National Standard for Information Sciences—Permanence of Paper for Printed Library Materials, ANSI Z329.48 ∞

Manufactured in the U.S.A.   AF 9-3577

01   00   99   98   97   1   2   3   4   5   6   7   8   9   10

To
Charlotte Blackham Bainton, my mother by blood,
Emily Blackham Bainton, her sister,
my mother in the spirit of adoption,
Mary Smith Woodruff, my mother-in-law—
All are mothers in love

CONTENTS

THE HOLY FAMILY

Martin Schongauer (1430–1491)

The stable is beneath the ruins of a Gothic arch.

Mary is kneeling and Joseph holding a lantern in accord with the

style typical after the fourteenth century.

Introduction

WHAT LUTHER HAS SAID about Christmas will affect the modern reader as diversely as the Christmas narrative itself. Some still believe in the opening of the heavens, the song of the angels, and the incredible star. They may nevertheless miss the wonder of God made flesh, but at least for them there is no barrier of rejected legend. For others the Christmas story is a fair and unbelievable tale, hallowed by the aura of a vanished faith. An Englishman of letters so describes his mood at midnight on a Christmas Eve, when he tuned in on his wireless and heard the Mass of the Nativity chanted by the monks of Appleworth. The ancient theme was rendered in an ancient tongue: *"Et subito erat cum angelo multitudo militiae caelestis laudentis Deum et dicentis, Gloria in excelsis et in terra pax . . .* And suddenly there was with the angel a multitude of the heavenly host praising God, and saying, Glory to God in the highest, and on earth peace . . ."

"There is no record in the world like this record," the listener reflected. If it were really true, "there would be no unsolved secret to elude mankind century after century." But what informed man can now believe that the heavens opened and the star appeared? The legends are gone, and with them the faith is also gone. "The tide of disruption is now at full flood." No compromise can arrest it. Modern man walks unguided through a bleak world, struggling convulsively until he finds a foothold in some new faith. The Christian story can fill him only with nostalgia for a loveliness irreparably lost.

Perhaps such a man might enjoy Luther as he would *The Green Pastures* or the Negro spirituals. They are so obviously naïve that the sophisticated can let himself go, and thus without loss of face or integrity can indulge a yearning for belief. To a degree any reader who enters into Luther at all will have to do so despite a rejection of some details. Even the most unquestioning person will scarcely take seriously his engaging fancy that God alternately turned on the star on and off to encourage or discipline the Wise Men. But one can smile or chuckle at his debonair embellishments without rejecting the essential message of the man. He was not himself primarily interested in miracles. "The Gospel," he once said, "is not so much a miracle as a marvel." Compared with his contemporaries, he was singularly parsimonious with regard to miracle.

The centuries immediately preceding had been marked by a lush growth of legend bolstering miracle by miracle. In order further to safeguard the sinlessness of Jesus, the doctrine of the Virgin birth was reinforced by that of the Immaculate Conception of the Virgin Mary. The possibility of defilement through birth was obviated by eliminating all the human marks of travail and weakness. The Virgin was represented, not as lying in bed after genuine labor, as in early Christian art, but as bearing painlessly and as kneeling directly thereafter in adoration of the Child. All creation recognized the wonder. Not only did Mary kneel but Joseph and the ox and ass as well. As the carol has it, "Ox and ass before Him bow." The wild animals likewise in the forest did obeisance. Not one star but three appeared in the heavens in honor of the Holy Trinity. In midwinter "there was a rose a-blooming." In the Annunciation the Angel Gabriel was portrayed bringing to the Virgin Mary a wedding contract to be signed by God the Father. He who takes delight in the stupendous should turn to the portrayals of the Nativity in late medieval woodcut and song.

Luther by comparison was very sober. His simplicity was due, of course, not to rationalism but to biblicism. He was not offended by miracle if it was in the sacred Word. But anything beyond the text of Scripture should be excised or at least subordinated. One might concede that Mary rode on a donkey from Nazareth to Bethlehem, but the Gospel does not say so. The Wise Men might have been three, but the number was merely an inference from the three gifts. There might equally have been half a dozen. Nor do we know that they arrived on the twelfth night. As for the legendary names of Melchior, Gaspar, and Balthasar, Luther never mentioned them at all.

The human rather than the miraculous aspects of the story interested him. At this point the Renaissance had in a measure paved the way. The artists had brought the whole scene closer home by portraying the biblical characters with the features of their contemporaries. The Virgin in Italy became *Ma Donna,* and the Babe, *Bambino.* The Wise Men were the aristocracy of Florence or of Venice, and the shepherds the peasants of the Apennines.

In the North, Mary became less comely because modeled on the maids of Flanders and of Germany. Joseph and the Wise Men grew more stocky and the Babe more plump. Halos sometimes were dropped. The simple pathos of a poor maid bringing forth her first-born in a cow stall was feelingly portrayed by Schongauer and Dürer in the woodcuts reproduced in this book.

Luther used some of the same devices. For him the setting was his own section of Germany. Palestine was removed to Thuringia, and the distance from Nazareth to Bethlehem was as that from Saxony to Franconia. In describing what Mary lacked for her lying-in, Luther gave a detailed picture of the appurtenances of childbirth in a German home. But it was in the field of emotion primarily that he invested the narrative with so deep a human quality. The distress of Mary, the misgiving of Joseph, the perplexity of the Wise Men, the cunning of Herod, all these are portrayed with the sort of human realism characteristic in our day of great historical novels like those of Thomas Mann, which develop biblical themes without ever caring whether they were in the first place literally so. Luther's interpretations of Christmas deserve reading, if for no other reason, because of the superb human delineations.

But these, of course, were not his chief concern, nor can they be for those who believe or would like to believe that something happened in Bethlehem's stable of extraordinary significance for the understanding of God. Christian teaching is that in Christ God became flesh. Compared with that, no particular miracle matters much. If one could but believe that God lay in the manger, one could let go the star and the angel's song and yet keep the faith. At this point Luther may help because he did not believe lightly.

He was simply amazed that all the characters in the Christmas story were themselves able to believe. He was able to compose the incredulous reflections of Mary, Joseph, the shepherds, and the Wise Men because these were precisely the doubts with which he was wrestling. The Virgin birth appeared to him a trivial miracle compared with the Virgin's faith.

Some may feel, however, that our difficulties are greater than his because he had not felt the impact of the new science. That is true enough. But Luther rightly discerned that the greatest difficulty does not lie at the point of science, new or old. The deepest incredibility for him was not mechanical but moral. The question was not whether God could or would make a special star, but why the Lord of all the universe should care enough about us mortals to take our flesh and share our woes. The condescension of God was the great wonder. This it is that reason cannot fathom. What man, if guided by his natural promptings, would do so much for another? Why should God humble himself to lie in the feedbox of a donkey and to hang upon a cross? The manger and the cross are never far apart for Luther. The birth was more than a lovely idyl. It took place in squalor and under the shadow of terror. Bethlehem presaged Calvary. Confronted by the self-emptying of God, modern man stands on no other ground than that of Luther. For neither can faith be easy. For neither need it be impossible. That Luther, feeling as acutely as we all the difficulties, could yet believe—this may help our unbelief.

His conception of the Nativity found expression in three forms: in sermon, in song, and in art. The most copious was preaching. Luther delivered between a hundred and fifty and two hundred sermons a year. He preached from two to four times on a Sunday and several times during the week at the university or in the household composed of children, servants, relatives, and student boarders. The Christmas theme might occupy him for more than a month out of the year, from the beginning of Advent on November 30 until Epiphany on January 6, the traditional date for the arrival of the three kings. In this book extracts have been selected from the sermons ranging over thirty years' time and have been woven together into a consecutive narrative and commentary. The material has been in a measure reconstructed by way of condensation, transposition, and paraphrase.

The second mode of expression for the Holy Night was song. Luther composed, in all, five carols, two of which are here translated afresh. The opening stanza of one of them appears within the border on page seventy. The other concludes this little book and calls for special mention. "From Heaven High" is the most childlike of all, and was almost certainly composed for Luther's own children. It was first published in 1535 and may well have been written the previous Christmas, when Hans was eight and Lenchen five. The carol is designed for a children's pageant in the church. Before the altar is placed a cradle with the Babe. On either side kneel Mary and Joseph. From the choir a chorister takes the part of the angel and makes the announcement:

"From heaven high I come to earth.
I bring you tidings of great mirth."

The shepherds and the children in the meantime have been standing just below the chancel steps. "Look now, you children,

at the sign" is their cue. At the close of this stanza the children take
up the song,

> *"How glad we'll be if it is so!*
> *With all the shepherds let us go."*

Singing they come forward around the cradle, and in unison
or singly take up the stanzas that exclaim over the baby Jesus and
invite him to be guest in their hearts. The closing stanza is sung by
all, angels, shepherds, children, and the entire audience. Luther was
sufficiently versed in music to be able to compose and set his own
tunes or to adapt old melodies to his words.

The reader will no doubt be puzzled over the omission from
this compilation of the beloved carol "Away in a Manger," commonly attributed to Martin Luther in our hymn books and
anthologies, often with realistic details of the Christmas tree in the
Luther home and the request of little Hans for a song. The legend
is doubly inaccurate, because the tree had not yet come to be asso-
ciated with Christmas in the Germany of Luther's day, and "Away
in a Manger" originated in Pennsylvania in connection with the
four hundredth anniversary of Luther's birth. It appeared first in
print in English in 1884. The earliest discoverable German version
is dated 1934, and is obviously a translation. Yet legends have not
only their beauty but also their truth. The ascription of the most
loved of all American carols to Martin Luther is a tribute, well
deserved, to the simplicity and tender pathos with which he
invested the theme.

Still another medium for the expression of Luther's ideas
about Christmas was pictorial. Here he was dependent upon

others. He could not wield the pen of the artist or the chisel of the woodcut carver, yet he was very much interested in the illustrations for his books, and gave directions to the artists. Yet strangely the Nativity, of which Luther was so fond, found scant representation in his works. One would expect to find it often among the five hundred or so woodcuts that adorned the editions of his Bible published during his lifetime. But among them all there is only a single Nativity, used as a decorative vignette on the title page to Ezekiel. One wonders why his publishers did not avail themselves of the extensive work of Dürer, Schongauer, Cranach, Altdorfer, and Holbein. The answer appears to be that biblical illustration had been conventionalized. The German Bibles of the late fifteenth and early sixteenth centuries are copiously decorated in the Old Testament and the Apocalypse, but have nothing for the remainder of the New Testament save the signs of the Evangelists and initial letters for the apostle Paul. Luther's printers during his lifetime did not venture to exceed the convention. After his death his pupil Veit Dietrich, in 1560, gave expression to Luther's vivid word pictures in an edition of his Bible richly illustrated throughout the Gospel story. But unfortunately the union of word and picture was not consummated at the moment when the arts of the woodcut and of translation were alike at the peak. Luther and Dürer never appeared together within the covers of a single work. This book seeks in slight measure to rectify the oversight, albeit in an alien tongue which can never quite convey the perfect flavor.

THOSE WHO SEEK the originals of these sermons will find the clue in the index to the sermon on the Gospels in the Weimar edition of Luther's works, volume XXII. The woodcuts are taken from:

Max Lehrs, ed., "Martin Schongauer," *Graphische Gesellschaft V* (Berlin, 1914), Plates II, III, IV.

Willy Kurth, ed., *The Complete Woodcuts of Albrecht Dürer,* (London, 1927), Nos. 182, 183, 185, 187, 219.

Johannes Luther, *Die Titeleinfassungen der Reformationszeit* (Leipzig, 1909). Page 75 is Leiferung I, No. 16.

Georg Jacob Wolf, "Albrecht Altdorfer," *Künstlermonografien* CXV (Bielefeld & Leipzig, 1925).

THE ANNUNCIATION

Martin Schongauer (1430-1491)

God the Father is above. The Spirit, as "the power of the Highest,"
in the form of a dove approaches Mary. The blossoming lily
symbolizes purity.

Annunciation

OUR LORD JESUS CHRIST was born of a line of ancestors whom the Evangelist Matthew arranges with artistry into three groups of fourteen patriarchs, fourteen kings, and fourteen princes. Among the latter were a number of disreputable characters, as we learn from the book of Kings, and there were no savory women. God holds before us this mirror of sinners that we may know that he is sent to sinners, and from sinners is willing to be born.

The way was paved for the ministry of our Lord by the forerunner, John the Baptist, who was born earlier than the Master. The father of John was named Zacharias and the mother Elisabeth, a kinswoman of the Virgin Mary. Zacharias was not the high priest, who officiated only once a year, but one of the minor priests who served for two weeks at a time in the Temple. During this period the priest was segregated from wife and family. Morning and evening he lighted the lamp while people prayed without.

The Angel Gabriel appeared to this Zacharias and announced that his wife should bear a son who should be called great in the sight of the Lord. He should drink neither wine nor strong drink. The angel announced further that John should turn many of the

Children of Israel to the Lord, which means that he would bring them to Christ. He was to become the forerunner.

The same angel was sent to make an even more amazing announcement to the Virgin Mary. We note that this angel was called Gabriel. The name means power. He was commander in chief of the heavenly host, the keeper of the sword, the marshal of the divine Majesty. A thousand angels were at his beck, and their radiance was more dazzling than a hundred suns. If angels were to speak to us in the majesty they enjoy in the presence of God, we could not endure the sight. The name "angel" means a messenger, and Gabriel, the chief, had already been used to carry a message to Zacharias. Why should God employ angels on such tasks? Could he not find a priest or prophet from Jerusalem or a preacher from Nazareth? The angels, though they are mighty princes in heaven, are not ashamed to be used as messengers, and Gabriel did not resent being used as an errand boy to carry word to a lowly maiden. His glory was laid aside, and he appeared to her simply in the guise of a comely youth.

The name of the maiden was Mary. The Hebrew form of the name is Miriam, and means "bitter myrrh." Why she was given this name I do not know, save that the Jews had the custom of naming children from the circumstances of the birth. Now the time when Christ should come was one of utter bitterness and extreme poverty for the Jews. They were a downtrodden people and their lot was pitiable, like ours today so that all might well weep bitterly.

Among the downtrodden people she was one of the lowliest, not a maid of high station in the capital city, but a daughter of a plain man in a small town. We may infer that she was of no account because she herself said in her song, "He hath regarded the low estate of his handmaiden." Who knows whether Joachim and Anna, her parents, were alive at the time? In all likelihood she was an orphan; nor is there the slightest ground for the legend that her parents were wealthy and divided the legacy into three portions, one for the Church, one for the poor, and one for Mary. In the village of Nazareth she appeared as a mere servant, tending the cattle and the house and no more esteemed that a maid among us who does her appointed chores. Her age was probably between thirteen and fifteen years.

And yet this was the one whom God chose. He might have gone to Jerusalem and picked out Caiaphas' daughter, who was fair, rich, clad in gold-embroidered raiment, and attended by a retinue of maids in waiting. But God preferred a lowly maid from a mean town.

Quite possibly Mary was doing the housework when the Angel Gabriel came to her. Angels prefer to come to people as they are fulfilling their calling and discharging their office. The angel appeared to the shepherds as they were watching their flocks, to Gideon as he was threshing the grain, to Samson's mother as she sat in the field. Possibly, however, the Virgin Mary, who was very religious, was in a corner praying for the redemption of Israel. During prayer, also, the angels are wont to appear.

The angel greeted Mary and said, "Hail, Mary, full of grace." That is the Latin rendering, which unhappily has been taken over literally into German. Tell me, is this good German? Would any German say you are full of grace? I have translated it, "Thou gracious one," but if I were really to write German, I would say,

"God bless you, dear Mary—*liebe Maria*," for any German knows that this word *liebe* comes right from the heart.

"Dear Mary," said the angel, "the Lord is with you. Blessed are you among women." We are unable to tell whether Mary perceived at once that it was an angel who spoke to her. Luke seems to imply that she did not, because he indicates that she was abashed, not so much by his appearance, as by his words. And they were most unusual: "O Mary, you are blessed. You have a gracious God. No woman has ever lived on earth to whom God has shown such grace. You are the crown among them all." These words so overwhelmed the poor child that she did not know where she was. Then the angel comforted her and said: "Fear not, Mary, for you have found favor with God, and, behold, you shall conceive in your womb and bring forth a son and you shall call his name Jesus. He shall be great and shall be called the Son of the Highest. And the Lord God shall give unto him the throne of his father David and he shall reign over the house of Jacob for ever; and of his kingdom there shall be no end."

To this poor maiden marvelous things were announced: that she should be the mother of the All Highest, whose name should be the Son of God. He would be a King and of his Kingdom there would be no end. It took a mighty reach of faith to believe that this baby would play such a role. Well might Mary have said, "Who am I, little worm, that I should bear a King?" She might have doubted, but she shut her eyes and trusted in God who could bring all things to pass, even though common sense were against it; and because she believed, God did to her as he had said. She was indeed troubled at first and inquired, "How can these things be, seeing that I know not a man?" She was flesh and blood, and for that reason, the angel reassured her, saying, "The Holy Ghost shall come upon you, and the power of the Highest shall overshadow you, and therefore also that holy thing which shall be born of you shall be called the Son of God."

We must both read and meditate upon the Nativity. If the meditation does not reach the heart, we shall sense no sweetness, nor shall we know what solace for humankind lies in this contemplation. The heart will not laugh nor be merry. As spray does not touch the deep, so mere meditation will not quiet the heart. There is such richness and goodness in this Nativity that if we should see and deeply understand, we should be dissolved in perpetual joy. Wherefore Saint Bernard declared there are here three miracles: that God and man should be joined in this Child; that a mother should remain a virgin; that Mary should have such faith as to believe that this mystery would be accomplished in her. The last is not the least of the three. The Virgin birth is a mere trifle for God; that God should become man is a greater miracle; but most amazing of all is that this maiden should credit the announcement that she, rather than some other virgin had been chosen to be the mother of God. She did indeed inquire of the angel, "How can these things be?" and he answered, "Mary, you have asked too high a question for me, but the Holy Spirit will come upon you and the power of the Most High will overshadow you and you will not know yourself how it happens." Had she not believed, she could not have conceived. She held fast to the word of the angel because she had become a new creature. Even so must we be transformed and renewed in heart from day to day. Otherwise Christ is born in vain. This is the word of the prophet: *"Unto us* a child is born, *unto us* a son is given"* (Isaiah 9:6). This is for us the hardest point, not so much to believe that He is the son of the Virgin and God himself, as to believe that this Son of God is ours. That is where we wilt, but he who does feel it has become another man. Truly it is marvelous in our eyes that God should place a little child in the lap of a virgin and that all our blessedness should lie in him. And this Child belongs to all mankind. God feeds the whole world through a Babe nursing at Mary's breast. This must be our daily exercise: to be transformed into Christ, being nourished by this food. Then will the heart be suffused with all joy and will be strong and confident against every assault.

THE VISITATION

Albrecht Dürer (1471-1528)

*A splendid example of Dürer's skill in the application of perspective
to landscape. Before his Lutheran conversion, Dürer sometimes showed
more interest in technique than in the theme.*

Visitation

THE ANGEL GABRIEL, after informing Mary that she was herself to become a mother while yet a virgin, conveyed the almost equally unbelievable news that her kinswoman Elisabeth had conceived in her old age and was already in her sixth month. Mary then arose "and went into the hill country with haste, into a city of Juda; and entered into the house of Zacharias, and saluted Elisabeth."

We observe that she went by the hill country, not by the plain. The journey would take her all of three days. We do not know the precise destination, for although Zacharias was a priest, he was not under the necessity of residing in Jerusalem. He was a poor priest, and we are not to think of Elisabeth as in a much more exalted station than Mary.

The Evangelist Luke advisedly inserted those words "with haste." Mary was full of faith, love, and modesty. When she knew that her cousin Elisabeth was with child, she had no peace until she had gone to her. She went with joy, love, and humility, but the chief reason was the word of the angel and that she believed it.

"And it came to pass, that, when Elisabeth heard the saluta-tion of Mary, the babe leaped in her womb; and Elisabeth was filled with the Holy Ghost: And she spake out with a loud voice, and said, Blessed art thou among women." Then Mary broke forth into singing. Her song is called the Magnificat because it begins with the words: "My soul doth magnify the Lord, and my spirit hath rejoiced in God my Saviour. For he hath regarded the low estate of his handmaiden."

They do Mary wrong who say that she gloried not in her virginity but in her humility. She gloried neither in her virginity nor in her humility, but solely in God's gracious regard. The stress should not be on the "low estate," but on the word "regarded." Her low estate is not to be praised, but God's regard, as, when a prince gives his hand to a beggar, the meanness of the beggar is not to be praised, but the graciousness and goodness of the prince. The evil eye looks only on the reward and the result of humility. The genuinely humble look not at the outcome of their humility. True humility does not know that it is humble. If it did, it would be proud from the contemplation of so fine a virtue.

Mary's song continued: "For, behold, from henceforth all generations shall call me blessed. For he that is mighty hath done to me great things; and holy is his name. And his mercy is on them that fear him from generation to generation. He hath showed strength with his arm; he hath scattered the proud in the imagination of the their hearts. He hath put down the mighty from their seats, and exalted on them of low degree."

God allows the godly to be powerless and oppressed so that everyone thinks they are done for, yet even in that very moment God is most powerfully present, though hidden and concealed. When the power of man fails, the power of God begins, provided faith is present and expectant. When the oppression is ended, then one sees what strength lies below the weakness. Even so was Christ powerless on the cross, and yet he was most mighty there and overcame sin, death, world, hell, devil, and all ill.

Mary's song went on: "He hath filled the hungry with good things; and the rich he hath sent empty away. He hath holpen his servant of Israel, in remembrance of his mercy; as he spake to our fathers, to Abraham, and to his seed for ever."

You have got to feel the pinch of hunger in the midst of scarcity and experience what hunger and scarcity are, when you do not know where to turn, to yourself, or to anyone else but only to God, that the work may be God's alone and of none other. You must not only think and speak of lowliness, but come into it, sink into it, utterly helpless, that God alone may save you. Or at any rate, should it not happen, you should at least desire it and not shrink. For this reason we are Christians and have the Gospel, that we may fall into distress and lowliness and that God thereby may have his work in us.

Mary stayed with Elisabeth about three months, and then returned to her own house.

See how purely she leaves all to God, and claims for herself no works, honor, or reputation. She behaves just as she did before any of this was hers—seeks no greater honor, is not puffed up, vaunts not herself, calls out to no one that she is the mother of God, but goes into the house and acts just as before—milks cows, cooks, scrubs the kettles, and sweeps the house like any housemaid or housemother in the most menial tasks, as if none of these overwhelming gifts and graces were hers. Among the other women and neighbors she was esteemed no more highly than before and did not ask to be. She was still a poor townswoman among the lowliest. What a simple pure heart was hers! What an amazing person she was! What mightiness was hidden below her lowliness! How many there were who met her, talked with her, ate and drank with her, and perhaps looked down upon her, who, had they known, would have been overpowered in her presence.

After Mary returned home, God put her to a severe trial. She was engaged to marry a man named Joseph and "before they came together, she was found with child of the Holy Ghost." The Scripture says that "Joseph her husband, being a just man, and not willing to make her a publick example, was minded to put her away privily. But while he thought on these things, behold, the angel of the Lord appeared to him in a dream, saying, Joseph, thou son of David, fear not to take unto thee Mary thy wife."

We can see from this that Mary was a poor little orphan, without father or mother, about fourteen years old. Joseph took pity on her and was betrothed to her lest she be deserted. If she had had parents alive, she would have been with them rather than a husband. She was a bride, but had not gone to live with her husband and still wore the garb of a virgin. Joseph intended to take her to wife, and was very much disturbed when he discovered that she was with child. She had spent the previous three months with Elisabeth. Joseph could hardly place a good construction upon her condition. If the like had happened to you or me, what should we have thought? Anyone in such a case would have said, "I won't have her even though she is a princess." Had Joseph wished to follow the letter of the law, he would have denounced her and she would have been stoned. This was a grievous cross to Mary that her bridegroom should suspect and cast her off. The Evangelist commends him for resolving to do it privily. He thought to himself, "She is a poor girl and if I expose her she will go from bad to worse." He did not wish to have any court proceedings which would be damaging to her, although he considered her hopeless. This holy virgin, celebrated by all the prophets, was judged by her own husband to be a loose woman. The holy maid could not come to honor before she had first been put to shame. Here she was, deserted by her husband, in danger of death, and with child. But God inclines his ear to all who call upon him. An angel came from heaven and said: "Fear not. There is no dishonor or disgrace. She is with child by the Holy Spirit." Joseph had nothing to go by save the Word of God and he accepted it. A godless man would have said it was just a dream, but Joseph believed the word of God and took unto him his wife.

Since Christ had to be born of a virgin, we may wonder why his mother married at all. Why was not her virginity proclaimed to all the world? This was done to obviate rumor. If Mary had come out and said that she was with child by the Holy Spirit and not by Joseph, she would have been put to death. She could not prove it, and no one would have believed it. It was against all Scripture, reason, and experience. Joseph kept the secret and became her servant, and none knew what the Holy Spirit was doing. Thus the married status proved a protection to a virgin.

Some claim, since Christ was born of a virgin, that virginity is superior to marriage. He did have to be born of a virgin that he might be a Saviour without sin. But take note that he was not born of a nun or a woman outside married status. Mary lived with her husband and no one supposed that they were any different from any other married people. Christ wished marriage to retain its honor alongside of the virginity of Mary. The virginity was concealed from the world; the marriage was proclaimed. Mary wore a veil like any other wife. If one would praise virginity, splendid, but not to the disparagement of marriage. Virginity, marriage, and widowhood do not earn heaven. They enter into heaven through faith in this little Child.

THE NATIVITY

Martin Schongauer (1430-1491)

On a distant hill a shepherd is listening to the song of three angels,
half human, half birdlike in form. Two shepherds approach.
The stable is beneath an improvised thatch over ruins.

Nativity

THE BIRTH OF CHRIST took place exactly when the Emperor Augustus sent out a decree that all the world should be taxed. This was no accident. The birth of Christ was timed to coincide with the census because God wanted to teach us the duty of obedience even to a heathen government. Had he been born prior to the census, it might have appeared that he was unwilling to be subject to the Roman Empire. At the very first moment of his life, Christ and his parents had to give evidence of obedience, not to God, but to the heathen emperor, the enemy of the Jews. This is the strongest proof that Christ's Kingdom is to be distinguished from that of the world. Christ did not wish to erect a kingdom like an earthly king, but wished to be subject to a heathen government. Is not this shameful, that Christ should obey a power that his people and his household regarded as an abomination? But Christ obeyed the civil government of the emperor. Every Christian, therefore, should let Augustus administer his realm— should not hinder but help.

But you say: "Government is not good. Since Christ did not wish to be a king, it is not good to govern. If it were, he would have accepted the proffered crown." If you are going to proceed on that premise, you will be a fine saint. If you wish to do just as Christ did, you will have to be born of a virgin, raise the dead, walk on water, take no wife, have no gold, nor any manservant or maidservant. You might as well say, "Nobody can be a Christian who has a wife and household, who is a peasant or a tailor, because Christ had no wife, trade, nor where to lay his head." Piffle to such confounded nonsense! Christ was a preacher. That is why he declined civil government. I am a preacher, too, and I decline it too. But I do not condemn civil government as wrong. It is wrong for me because I am not called to it. I might as well say that no one should be a householder, for is not a householder a prince, king, emperor, and bishop over servants, maids, and children? "Very well," say our radicals, "leave wife and child, because they do involve government." But how are you going to have a higher power if you do not have a lower? How can you have a town counselor without townsmen? But many townsmen make a city, and many cities make a principality and so on up to a kingdom and an empire. Although Christ was no civil ruler, he did not forbid civil rule. Do not take everything that Christ did as an example. In that case you might say to me, "Dr. Martin won't be a burgomaster, judge, or hand worker, so these are not Christian professions." If I had to do them all, they would break my back. But you are not to look at what Christ did or at what I do. God gives to each his own task. You might as well say, "My wife wears a veil and she is a Christian, so I must wear a veil to be a Christian." Nonsense! But Christ remains a preacher, Augustus an emperor, and the shepherds remain shepherds.

The law of the census required that each householder must be present in his home at the time of the enrollment. Joseph was of the lineage of David and had to go to Bethlehem, the city of David. Despite his royal ancestry, he was so poor that he had been unable to make a living in Judea and for that reason had transferred to Nazareth. Now he had to go back. Scripture says that he took with him "Mary his espoused wife, being great with child." She would have had good reason to excuse herself from making the journey so close to her time, but she said nothing because she wished to trouble no one. We can see how poor Joseph must have been that he could not afford to hire some old woman or neighbor to stay with Mary and look after her while he was gone.

How unobtrusively and simply do those events take place on earth that are so heralded in heaven! On earth it happened in this wise: There was a poor young wife, Mary of Nazareth, among the meanest dwellers of the town, so little esteemed that none noticed the great wonder that she carried. She was silent, did not vaunt herself, but served her husband, who had no man or maid. They simply left the house. Perhaps they had a donkey for Mary to ride upon, though the Gospels say nothing about it and we may well believe that she went on foot. Think how she was treated in the inns on the way, she who might well have been taken in a golden carriage, with gorgeous equipage! How many great ladies and their daughters there were at that time, living in luxury, while the mother of God, on foot, in midwinter trudged her weight across the fields! How unequal it all was!

The journey was certainly more than a day from Nazareth in Galilee to Bethlehem, which lies on the farther side of Jerusalem.

Joseph had thought, "When we get to Bethlehem, we shall be among relatives and can borrow everything." A fine idea that was!

Bad enough that a young bride married only a year could not have had her baby at Nazareth in her own house instead of making all that journey of three days when heavy with child. The inn was full. No one would release a room to this pregnant woman. She had to go to a cow stall and there bring forth the Maker of all creatures because nobody would give way.

"And so it was, that, while they were there, the days were accomplished that she should be delivered. And she brought forth her firstborn son, and wrapped him in swaddling clothes, and laid him in a manger."

When now they were come to Bethlehem, the Evangelist says that they were, of all, the lowest and the most despised, and must make way for everyone until they were shoved into a stable to make a common lodging and table with the cattle, while many cutthroats lounged like lords in the inn. They did not recognize what God was doing in the stable. With all their eating, drinking, and finery, God left them empty, and this comfort and treasure was hidden from them. Oh, what a dark night it was in Bethlehem that this light should not have been seen. Thus shows God that he has no regard for what the world is and has and does. And the world shows that it does not know or consider what God is and has and does.

Joseph had to do his best, and it may well be that he asked some maid to fetch water or something else, but we do not read that anyone came to help. They heard that a young wife was lying in a cow stall and no one gave heed. Shame on you, wretched Bethlehem! The inn ought to have burned with brimstone, for even though Mary had been a beggar maid or unwed, anybody at such a time should have been glad to give her a hand.

There are many of you in this congregation who think to yourselves: "If only I had been there! How quick I would have been to help the Baby! I would have washed his linen. How happy I would have been to go with the shepherds to see the Lord lying in the manger!" Yes, you would! You say that because you know how great Christ is, but if you had been there at that time you would have done no better than the people of Bethlehem. Childish and silly thoughts are these! Why don't you do it now? You have Christ in your neighbor. You ought to serve him, for what you do to your neighbor in need you do to the Lord Christ himself.

The birth was still more pitiable. No one regarded this young wife bringing forth her firstborn. No one took her condition to heart. No one noticed that in a strange place she had not the very least thing needful in childbirth. There she was without preparation: no light, no fire, in the dead of night, in the thick darkness. No one came to give the customary assistance. The guests swarming in the inn were carousing, and no one attended to this woman. I think myself if Joseph and Mary realized that her time was so close she might perhaps have been left in Nazareth. And now think what she could use for swaddling clothes—some garment she could spare, perhaps her veil—certainly not Joseph's breeches which are now on exhibition at Aachen.

She ". . . wrapped him in swaddling clothes, and laid him in a manger." Why not in a cradle, on a bench, or on the ground? Because they had no cradle, bench, table, board, nor anything whatever except the manger of the oxen. That was the first throne of this King. There in a stable, without man or maid, lay the Creator of all the world. And there was the maid of fifteen years bringing forth her firstborn without water, fire, light, or pan, a sight for tears! What Mary and Joseph did next, nobody knows. The scholars say they adored. They must have marveled that this Child was the Son of God. He was also a real human being. Those who say that Mary was not a real mother lose all joy. He was a true baby, with flesh, blood, hands, and legs. He slept, cried, and did everything else that a baby does only without sin.

Think, women, there was no one there to bathe the baby. No warm water, nor even cold. No fire, no light. The mother was herself midwife and the maid. The cold manger was the bed and the bathtub. Who showed the poor girl what to do? She had never had a baby before. I am amazed that the little one did not freeze. Do not make of Mary a stone. It must have gone straight to her heart that she was so abandoned. She was flesh and blood, and must have felt miserable—and Joseph too—that she was left in this way, all alone, with no one to help, in a strange land in the middle of winter. Her eyes were moist even though she was happy, and aware that the baby was God's Son and the Saviour of the world. She was not stone. For the higher people are in the favor of God, the more tender are they.

Mary was not only holy. She was also the mother of the Lord. With trembling and reverence, before nestling him to herself, she laid him down, because her faith said to her, "He will be the Son of the Highest.'" No one else on earth had this faith, not even Joseph, for although he had been informed by the angel the word did not go to his heart as to the heart of Mary, the mother.

Let us, then, meditate upon the Nativity just as we see it happening in our own babies. I would not have you contemplate the deity of Christ, the majesty of Christ, but rather his flesh. Look upon the baby Jesus. Divinity may terrify man. Inexpressible majesty will crush him. That is why Christ took on our humanity, save for sin, that he should not terrify us but rather that with love and favor he should console and confirm.

Behold Christ lying in the lap of his young mother, still a virgin. What can be sweeter than the Babe, what more lovely than the mother! What fairer than her youth! What more gracious than her virginity! Look at the Child, knowing nothing. Yet all that is belongs to him, that your conscience should not fear but take comfort in him. Doubt nothing. Watch him springing in the lap of the maiden. Laugh with him. Look upon this Lord of Peace and your spirit will be at peace. See how God invites you in many ways. He places before you a babe with whom you may take refuge. You cannot fear him, for nothing is more appealing to man than a babe. Are you affrighted? Then come to him, lying in the lap of the fairest and sweetest maid. You will see how great is the divine goodness, which seeks above all else that you should not despair. Trust him! Trust him! Here is the Child in whom is salvation. To me there is no greater consolation given to mankind than this, that Christ became man, a child, a babe, playing in the lap and at the breasts of his most gracious mother. Who is there whom this sight would not comfort? Now is overcome the power of sin, death, hell, conscience, and guilt, if you come to judge this gurgling Babe and believe that he is come, not to judge you, but to save.

THE SHEPHERDS

Albrecht Dürer (1471-1528)

The stable is a thatched ruin of Romanesque architecture to suggest the
remote. The ox and ass feed in the rear of the stable. Shepherds arrive
with bagpipes. Cherubim at the manager contracted Luther's view.

Shepherds

"AND THERE WERE in the same country shepherds abiding in the field, keeping watch over their flock by night."

That was a mean job, watching flocks by night. Common sense calls it low-down work, and the men who do it are regarded as trash. But the Evangelist lauds the angels because they proclaimed their message only to shepherds watching their flock by night. These were real sheepherders. And what did they do? They did what real shepherds should do. They stayed in their station and did the work of their calling. They were pure in heart and content with their work, not aspiring to be townsmen or nobles, nor envious of the mighty. Next to faith this is the highest art—to be content with the calling in which God has placed you. I have not learned it yet.

Who would have thought that men whose job was tending unreasoning animals would be so praised that not a pope or a bishop is worthy to hand them a cup of water? It is the very devil that no one wants to follow the shepherds. The married man wants to be without a wife, or the nobleman to be a prince. It is: "If I were this! If I were that!" You fool! The best job is the one you have. If you are married, you cannot have a higher status. If you are a servant, you are in the very best position. Be diligent and know that there are no greater saints on this earth than servants. Do not say, "If I were"; say, "I am."

Look at the shepherds. They were watching their flocks by night, and an angel came and made them apostles, prophets, and children of God. Caiaphas, Herod, and the high priests were not deemed worthy. I would rather be one of those shepherds than that the Pope should make me a saint or the emperor make me a king.

"And, lo, the angel of the Lord came upon them, and the glory of the Lord shone round about them: and they were sore afraid."

The field was flooded with light—brilliant, dazzling. Not the town, but the field was lighted up. Why did not the angel go to Jerusalem? There was the worship established by God. There were the princes of the people and the rulers in the Church and State. There were the Temple and the high priests ordained of God. Why did not the angel go to them? He went to Bethlehem, a dung heap compared with Jerusalem, as Pratau is compared with Nürnberg. And he did not go to the town of Bethlehem but to the shepherds.

"And the angel said unto them, Fear not: for, behold, I bring you good tidings of great joy, which shall be to all people."

This joy is not just for Peter and Paul, but for all people. Not just to apostles, prophets, and martyrs does God say, but to you, "Come, see the baby Jesus."

"Fear not," said the angel. I fear death, the judgment of God, the world, hunger, and the like. The angel announces a Saviour who will free us from fear. Not a word is said about our merits and works, but only of the gift we are to receive.

"For unto you is born this day," that is, *unto us.* For our sakes he has taken flesh and blood from a woman, that his birth might become our birth. I too may boast that I am a son of Mary. This is the way to observe this feast—that Christ be formed in us. It is not enough that we should hear his story if the heart be closed. I must listen, not to a history, but to a gift. If I tell you that someone on a certain mountain peak has picked up a hundred gulden, you will say, "What is that to me?" But if you are the one who has picked it up, you will be joyful. What is it to me if someone else has goods, honors, riches, and a pretty wife? That does not touch the heart. But if you hear that this Child is yours, that takes root, and a man becomes suddenly so strong that to him death and life are the same.

"And this shall be a sign unto you; Ye shall find the babe wrapped in swaddling clothes, lying in a manger."

This is God's wedding. Where is the castle? A cow stall, a manger, with an ox and an ass, a fine bridal bed, fit to lay a dog in! But the angels are not ashamed of it. "Ye shall find {him} . . . lying in a manger."

The only present you need to bring to this wedding is a happy heart. God smiles and all the host of heaven rejoices.

"And suddenly there was with the angel a multitude of the heavenly host."

An innumerable multitude! There are more angels in heaven than blades of grass in all the gardens in the whole world. So many men have never lived on earth as there are angels in heaven. You would think that some of these angels might have gone to the baby Jesus to take him a golden cradle or a feather bed or some warm water. And why didn't they? They were singing that he is the Lord and Saviour. Why, then, did they not go to lend him a hand? That is something we cannot understand. We shall simply have to believe it until we find out at the resurrection.

They were "praising God, and saying, Glory to God in the highest."

See what God did in heaven about this birth which the world despised and did not even see and know. The joy was so great that the angels could not stay in heaven, but had to break out and tell man on earth. The angels proclaimed to the shepherds "tidings of great joy." This is a mighty comfort to us. What the world despised the angels honored. They would have had a much bigger celebration if God had allowed them, but he wished to teach us through his Son to despise the pomp of the world.

All the angels in heaven, not one excepted, sang, "Glory to God in the highest." What a shame that all men should not preach this word when all the angels in heaven play it on organs and pipes in eternity! The angels had no bigger congregation than two shepherds in a field. They were filled with too great joy for words. And we who hear this message, "Behold, I bring you good tidings," never feel one spark of joy. I hate myself because when I see him laid in a manger, in the lap of his mother, and hear the angels sing, my heart does not leap into flame. With what good reason should we all despise ourselves that we remain so cold when this word is spoken to us over which all men should dance and leap and burn for joy! We act as though it were a frigid, historical fact that does not smite our hearts, as if someone were merely relating that the sultan has a crown of gold.

"And on earth peace," sang the angels, "good will toward men."

The Kingdom of Christ is a proclamation of peace and grace, as the angels sang that he should be the Saviour of the whole world to free his people and save them from their sins. That he has done and still is doing. He is not the sort of Lord who fights with the sword and has to do with civil government. Rather he rules with the gracious preaching of peace. For that reason he is called Jesus, meaning a Saviour who helps his people to turn and be saved. We have often explained, and explain again, how to understand the Kingdom of our Lord; how to distinguish the spiritual and the temporal realms; that this Lord Christ does not build castles, towns, and villages like an emperor, king, or elector of Saxony, or even like me in my own household, but he saves his people from their sins. This is a fair, dear, and precious assurance to troubled and tormented consciences laden with sins, that to them and to us all a Child is born who will rule and vindicate, who will help and not destroy, murder, strangle, or kill.

These are not the words of man. This preaching is from heaven and, God be praised, it is communicated also to us, for it is just the same to hear and read this preaching as to receive it from an angel. The shepherds did not see the angels. They saw only a great light and heard the word of the angel, just as one can hear it now or read it in a book, if eyes and ears are open to learn and rightly to use. If one does not know the baby Jesus, it is impossible that one should rightly honor God. Because men do not know and revere this Child, they rage and devour each other. Where this Child is accepted there will be plenty and healing upon earth. For what is it like where Christ is not? What is the world if not a downright hell and nothing but lying, greed, gluttony, drunkenness, adultery, assault, and murder, that is, the very devil? Friends can no more be trusted than foes. But those who hear the angels sing, who know and receive the baby Jesus and give due honor to God, are like gods to their fellow men, peaceable, kind folk, glad to help and counsel anyone. When God is honored, then are men friendly, without hate and envy, each regarding the other as greater than himself and saying, "Dear brother, pray for me."

"And it came to pass, as the angels were gone away from them into heaven, the shepherds said to one another, Let us now go even to Bethlehem, and see this thing which is come to pass, which the Lord hath made known to us."

This is a great miracle that the shepherds should have believed this message. They might easily have thought to themselves, "Are we two shepherds worthy that the whole host of heaven should be marshaled for us and all the kings on the earth and the dwellers in Jerusalem be passed by?" I know I would have appealed to common sense and I would have said: "Who am I compared to God and angels and kings? It is an apparition." But the Holy Spirit, who preached through the angels, caused the shepherds to believe. They were so strong in the faith that they were worthy to be spoken to by angels and to hear every angel in heaven singing a cantata just for them. This is a pure wonder that enters not into the heart of man. Our God begins with angels and ends with shepherds. Why does he do such preposterous things? He puts a Babe in a crib. Our common sense revolts and says, "Could not God have saved the world some other way?" I would not have sent an angel. I would simply have called the devil and said, "Let my people go." The Christian faith is foolishness. It says that God can do anything and yet makes him so weak that either his Son had no power or wisdom or else the whole story is made up. Surely the God who in the beginning said: "Let there be light," "Let there be a firmament," "Let the dry land appear," could have said to the devil, "Give me back my people, my Christians." God does not even send an angel to take the devil by the nose. He sends, as it were, an earthworm lying in weakness, helpless, without his mother, and he suffers him to be nailed to a cross. The devil says, "I will judge him." So spoke Caiaphas and Pilate, "He is nothing but a carpenter," and then in his weakness and infirmity he crunches the devil's back and alters the whole world. He suffered himself to be trodden under the foot of man and to be crucified, and through weakness he takes the power and the Kingdom.

"And . . . {the shepherds} came with haste, and found Mary, and Joseph, and the babe lying in a manger."

God is amazing. The Babe is in a manger, not worthy of a cradle or a diaper, and yet he is called Saviour and Lord. The angels sing about him, and the shepherds hear and come and honor him whom no maid serves as he lies with an ox and an ass. If I had come to Bethlehem and seen it, I would have said: "This does not make sense. Can this be the Messiah? This is sheer nonsense." I would not have let myself be found inside the stable.

"And when they had seen it, they made known abroad the saying which was told them concerning this child. And all they that heard it wondered at those things which were told them by the shepherds. But Mary kept all these things, and pondered them in her heart."

Here we see that the preaching and singing of the angel were not in vain. However much the shepherds loved their sheep, they went at once to see the Babe, whom the angels called the Lord. This is the first fruit, that they followed the word of the angel. The second is that they all became preachers themselves and told everybody what they had learned from this Child, for the Evangelist says, "And all they that heard it wondered at those things which was told them by the shepherds." Yes, but they did not remember them very long. For a quarter of a year anyone could have told how the Child had been born at Bethlehem, how the angels sang and the Wise Men came from the East. But two, three, or four years afterward everyone had forgotten. And when the Lord came to baptism at the age of thirty, no one remembered a thing about it.

"But Mary kept all these things, and pondered them in her heart." She wrote them in her heart, meditated upon them, and thought to herself, "This is wonderful news that I am the mother of the Child whom the angels call Lord." These thoughts sank so deeply into her heart that she would have held to them though the whole world were against her.

Why did she ponder these things in her heart? Because she too was in need of preaching. Even though she was the mother and had borne the Child, she had need to ponder these words in her heart, in order to strengthen her faith and increase her assurance. She reflected how these words corresponded to those of the angel: "He shall be great, and shall be called the Son of the Highest." The message of the angels fitted in exactly with the annunciation by Gabriel. This was to her a great joy and confirmation. Without these a human heart would have difficulty in believing: "I am the mother of the King of Kings lying here in the manger." There was nothing kingly about the Babe, but Mary heard from the shepherds that he was the Saviour of the world and greater than all kings, and that she should be his mother and nurse him. The quality of faith in this Virgin no words can express. If anyone has faith and thinks he knows enough, let him take a lesson from this mother and let him assemble the passages of Scripture in order to confirm his faith. If he has one passage, good, but if he has eight or ten, that is better.

When I die I see nothing but sheer blackness except for this light: "Unto you is born this day . . . a Saviour." The Saviour will help me when all else fails. When the heaven, the stars, and all the creatures glower, I see nothing in earth and heaven but this Child. This light should be so great in my eyes that I can say: "Dear Mary, you have borne this Child not for yourself alone. You are indeed his mother. But I have an even greater honor than yours as mother. Your honor is the bearing of the body of this Child, but my honor is this, that you have my treasure, and I know no one, man or angel, who can help me as can the Babe that you, dear Mary, hold in your lap." If, for the sake of this Child, a man could count all gold and goods, all power and honor as blackness; if, compared with this Child, the stars in heaven and all the treasures of earth were as nothing, then he would know the true use of the angel's message.

Enough has been said on the use and fruit of the birth of Christ. The sum of it is all here: "Unto you is born this day . . .

a Saviour." Let us look for a moment at the spiritual significance. Mary is the figure of Christianity, that is, all Christians who wrap the newborn Child in the word of the Gospel. The swaddling clothes signify the preaching of the Gospel; the manger signifies the place where Christians come together to hear the word of God. The ox and the ass stand for us.

"And the shepherds returned, glorifying and praising God for all the things that they had heard and seen, as it was told unto them."

This is wrong. We should correct this passage to read, "They went and shaved their heads, fasted, told their rosaries, and put on cowls." Instead we read, "The shepherds returned." Where to? To their sheep. Oh, that can't be right! Did they not leave everything and follow Christ? Must not one forsake father and mother, wife and child, to be saved? But the Scripture says plainly that they returned and did exactly the same work as before. They did not despise their service, but took it up again where they left off with all fidelity and I tell you that no bishop on earth ever had so fine a crook as those shepherds.

SLAUGHTER OF THE INNOCENTS

Albrecht Altdorfer (1480-1538)

The building is a ruin of Renaissance architecture. The soldier
is attired as a German mercenary of Luther's day.

Herod

"NOW WHEN JESUS was born in Bethlehem of Judea in the days of Herod the king, behold, there came Wise Men from the east to Jerusalem, saying, Where is he that is born King of the Jews? for we have seen his star in the east, and are come to worship him."

This Gospel is a terror to the great, learned, holy, and powerful because they all despise Christ. It is a comfort to the lowly to whom alone Christ is revealed.

The announcers of this event are commonly called the three kings, perhaps because of the three gifts. We may let the simple have it so and it does not matter much, though we are not told in Scripture whether there were two, three, or how many. We may safely assume that they came from Arabia, or Sheba. This may be inferred from the presents of gold, frankincense, and myrrh, all of which are found in that land. We are not to suppose that they purchased them elsewhere, because the custom of the East is to make presents from the best fruit of the land. Nor should we assume with the painters that one of the Wise Men brought gold, another frankincense, and a third myrrh, but each brought all.

The Gospel calls them Magi—not so much prophets as magicians, masters of secret lore. They were not wizards in league with the devil, but experts in the properties of nature, like the alchemists who can turn copper into gold. Such secret knowledge of nature was given by God's Spirit to Jacob and Solomon, and was in great vogue in Persia and Arabia. It is a noble art and has produced many wise men. But the art degenerated into necromancy and has been so abused by the devil that the name "magician" has fallen into disrepute.

These Magi, or Wise Men, were not kings, but learned men in the art of nature. Without doubt they dabbled also in superstitions, for they allowed themselves to be guided entirely by the course of the star. They were like philosophers in Greece, the priests in Egypt, or the professors in our universities. Hidden away in their lore is something of Christ and the way of life. These studies are no longer being cultivated in our universities, and the peasants know more about them than the doctors who have become the devil's mockingbirds. The Wise Men may be called natural scientists from the East, or professors of natural science from Arabia.

Some have wondered how they could cover so great a distance in so few days. The tradition is that they arrived on Twelfthnight, whereas the geographers reckon a sixty-day journey from the chief city of Arabia to the coast of the Mediterranean, which lies only three German miles beyond Bethlehem. Such matters do not bother me. It is no article of faith to believe that they arrived on Twelfth-night, and for that matter they need not have started from the chief city of Arabia. They could have found Mary twenty or thirty days after the birth because she was required by law, like any other woman, to stay in Bethlehem for purification at the end of six weeks. Still I will not quarrel with the common belief in a miracle so long as it is not made into an article of faith and enforced. That which is not written in God's Word does not need to be regarded as an article of faith. The point of the Gospels is that the prophecy was fulfilled at the birth of Christ under the first foreign prince, Herod, and that the stargazers out of the East came a long journey to worship him when the priests and the learned of his own land declined.

Some say that since the Wise Men were taught by a star, we should all be stargazers. Well, of course, we must observe the sun sufficiently to recognize sunrise, midday, and sunset, and similarly the moon and the stars by night. The weather must be studied for plowing and reaping, but there is no need to know the size of the sun, its distance from the earth, or what power it has over gold and the like. Comets and eclipses must be recognized as signs of the wrath of God and that is enough.

The star was simply a sign to the Magi, and the astrologers are not in a position to base their art upon this passage of the Gospels. The Wise Men did not try to cast Christ's horoscope. They simply saw that this was a sign of a great king and they asked only where he was. In order to give no comfort to the astrologers, Christ made a brand-new star as a sign of his birth. How the Magi knew that this star meant the birth of a king is more than I know. But I don't see any great miracle here. The Arabians were descended from Abraham, whose sons by Keturah dwelt in the East. Abraham was very well-informed because God said, "How can I conceal what I am doing from Abraham?" He would surely have passed on this knowledge, not only to Isaac, but also to his other sons. Thus from the sons of Abraham the Wise Men could know that a king was to be born among the Jews, particularly when they saw his star over Judea.

They could not have been so very far distant if they were to see it—not more than four days' journey. How could they have supposed that the star was over Jerusalem if they had been so far away as commonly thought? Very probably they were close to the border of Judea near Egypt, otherwise, they could not have seen the star, especially since it must have been low in the heavens. Had it been high like an ordinary star, men ten miles apart would equally have supposed it to be directly over them. Since it was able to stop, not merely over the town, but over the very house, it must have been low. It was a star especially created for this very purpose, and not like other stars that traverse the heavens. This star stopped by night when the Wise Men were camping and in the morning ambled along at the pace they were riding.

When the Wise Men received the divine revelation that the king of the Jews was born, they made straight for Jerusalem, for, of course, they expected to find him at the capital in a lordly castle and a golden chamber. Where else would common sense expect to find a king? But because they were so sure of themselves, the star left them. Then they were sorely tried, and had they relied solely on human wisdom, would surely have said: "Confound it! We have come all this way for nothing. The star has deceived us. The devil has led us by an apparition. If a king had been born, would he not be in the capital and in a palace? But when we come, the star disappears and we find no one who knows anything about him. Can it be that we foreigners should be the first to have news of him in the royal city? Everyone is so cold and unfriendly that no one offers to go with us and show us the child. They do not believe themselves that to them a king is born, and shall we come and find him? How desolate for the birth of a king! If a puppy were born there would be some little stir, and here a king is supposed to be born and everything is so still. One of our shepherds makes more fuss over the birth of a babe, and when a cow calves more people know about it than have heard of this king. Should not the people be singing, capering, lighting lamps and torches, bedecking the streets with roses and mayflowers? What a miserable king we are seeking! What fools we have been to let ourselves start on this quest!" Nature wants to feel and be certain before believing, but grace will believe before she feels. Faith steps gaily into the darkness, trusting simply in the Word.

But having come, they decided to inquire of the king before returning. At their report, Herod the king "was troubled, and all Jerusalem with him." Why was Herod terrified and all Jerusalem with him? *He* had good reason to be afraid because he had tyrannized over the Jews for thirty years. Though a foreigner, he was acquainted with the prophecy that the scepter should not depart from Jacob, and now that the time was fulfilled, he trembled and thought to himself: "I have been king for thirty years and now the people are getting ready to oust me and these foreigners come and ask openly in the city for the newborn king. That sounds bad."

But why was all Jerusalem troubled with him? The Jews feared that Herod and the Romans would shed much blood if there were a new king. They had resisted Herod and Rome on earlier occasions and had been crushed, and they trusted more to the arm of man than to God.

Then Herod "gathered all the chief priests and scribes of the people together, . . . {and} demanded of them where Christ should be born." Herod, the rascal, was quite religious. Outwardly he did everything that a good man should. He called in the Wise Men, the priests and scribes, but he showed his heart later when he murdered the innocents.

"And they said unto him, In Bethlehem of Judea: for thus it is written by the prophet, And thou Bethlehem, in the land of Juda, art not the least among the princes of Juda: for out of thee shall come a Governor, that shall rule my people Israel."

Now Herod had a crafty plan. "The Jews," thought he, "will hide the truth from me, but I will find out the town where this king is to be born and also the time, and then if they hide him, I will catch him anyway. I will kill so many babies that he cannot escape." So he called the scribes to him and said, "Where is Christ to be born?" Then perhaps through fear, the scribes answered him that in the Prophet Micah it is written that He should be born in Bethlehem.

Why did the star not take the Wise Men straight to Bethlehem without any necessity of consulting the Scriptures? Because God wanted to teach us that we should follow the Scriptures and not our own murky ideas.

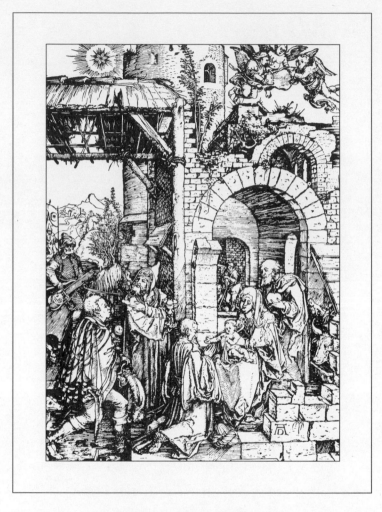

THE ADORATION OF THE WISE MEN

Albrecht Dürer (1471-1528)

The cherubim on the roof are observed only by the ass.

The architecture is again Romanesque.

Wise Men

"THEN HEROD, when he had privily called the Wise Men, enquired of them diligently what time the star appeared. And he sent them to Bethlehem, and said, Go and search diligently for the young child; and when ye have found him, being me word again, that I may come and worship him also."

We can see from this text that these Wise Men were not kings and princes, but merely honorable men like our professors and preachers. Herod treated them as subjects when he commanded them to go to Bethlehem and bring him word. He would not have done this if they had been kings or lords. He would have invited them to dine and would have accompanied them on their way with royal treatment, for all histories say that Herod was a smooth man who observed the etiquette of courts. Since he summoned them secretly, they must have been of much lower station. And why secretly—was not all the land his and under his control? Because he knew well that the Jews hated him, and had the interview been public, they might have sought to induce the Wise Men to mislead him that the new king might slip through his fingers. He inquired as to the exact appearance of the star because he had already made up his mind to slaughter the innocents. He thought to himself: "If a new king is born, the Jews will be glad. They will hide him until he is grown up, then they will bring him to light and kill me. Therefore, I must get ahead of them and inquire warily. If he is hidden, I will catch him anyway by killing all of the children at the same time." To carry out this crafty decision he represented himself to the Magi as very humble and reverent and desirous of worshiping him.

"When they had heard the king, they departed; and, lo, the star, which they saw in the east, went before them, till it came and stood over where the young child was. When they saw the star, they rejoiced with exceeding great joy."

Now the Wise Men had the faith to follow the word of the Prophet Micah. They were not offended that the king was not born in Jerusalem. They left the Temple and went to the cow stall.

If I had been there, I would have stayed in the Temple and said: "God dwells here and if the Child is to be found anywhere in the world, it will be where all the priests are gathered and God is served." We may profit from the example of these heathen, who took no offense when directed from Jerusalem, the great city, to little Bethlehem. They followed the Word, and God comforted them by putting back the star, which led them now to Bethlehem and to the very door where the young Child lay.

Here the Evangelist shows us the true nature of faith, how they believed simply what they had not seen and held fast to the Word. That is why God brought them from their land to where they should hear the Word, but God let them first fall into error and bewilderment. They thought the Child would be born in the capital, Jerusalem, and that is where they went. Then the star left them, and no one in the city so much as knew that a king was to be born. The Wise Men supposed that he would be born in circumstances of pomp like the son of a potentate. God did not leave them long in their error but showed them through the Scripture that they would not find him as they supposed in the big city, but in a little village, and he directed them to the royal town of Bethlehem. This was a grievous cross to the Wise Men. Common sense said to them: "You are fools to have made this long journey at the behest of a star. Everything at the capital is still. No one knows anything about it. The people tell us to go to Bethlehem and we do not know whether we shall find him there."

You will notice that none of the Jerusalemites went along. They left the Babe to lie where he was and did not go to him, though they might well have done so from the ends of the earth. But they let these foreigners go to find out where he was, while they neglected him through fear of the tyrant Herod.

Faith, however, pays no regard to what it sees and feels, but clings only to the Word. The Wise Men were cast down and offended. They had started out in the confident expectation of finding him, and as a matter of fact found nothing. The Evangelist makes plain how rebuffed they felt when he says, "When they saw the star, they rejoiced with exceeding great joy." It is as if he had said, "When the star reappeared, they were very happy and thought: 'It is right after all. We were not deceived.'" We must do the same thing and hold fast to the Word.

This struggle the Wise Men passed through, and because they believed the word of the prophet, God sent the star again, more friendly than the first time. It was close to them as their guide.

They were certain now and did not need to ask the way. The first time it was afar off and they were not sure where they would find the King. It is always so with the Christian man. After a spiritual struggle, God is so heartfelt, so near and clear, that not only does a man forget the anguish and the struggle but they are endeared to him. And now he is so strong that he is no longer offended by the lowliness of Christ, for he has come to see that he who would find Christ must be ready to find only shame, as the Magi were ashamed when the star failed. Their joy on the reappearance shows that they had suffered no little shock, and when they came through the struggle they were newborn for delight and no longer offended in Christ.

"And when they were come into the house, they saw the young child with Mary his mother, and fell down, and worshipped him: and when they had opened their treasures, they presented unto him gifts; gold, and frankincense, and myrrh."

Though they saw but a tumbled down shack and a poor young mother with a poor little babe, not like a king at all, meaner than one of their own servants, they did not shrink, but in great, strong faith cast out all misgivings of common sense, and, following simply the word of the prophet and the witness of the star, they accepted him for a king, fell on their knees, worshiped him, and presented their treasures. The world would not have done so, but according to her wont would have looked for a velvet cushion and a host of servants and maids. The world makes presents to those who already have enough, and, to provide them, snatches the bread from the mouths of the hungry who have nothing but what they earn with their bloody sweat.

If we Christians would join the Wise Men, we must close our eyes to all that glitters before the world and look rather on the despised and foolish things, help the poor, comfort the despised, and aid the neighbor in his need. Do not boast that you have built churches and endowed masses. God will say: "What to me are your churches and masses? What do I care about your altars and your bells? Do I take pleasure in stone and wood? Is not the heaven my throne and the earth the footstool of my feet? Who told you to build churches? I have set before you spiritual temples. These you should build, feed, and help, but you have gone about doing foolish things which I commanded not. I know you not."

Let us then observe how these Wise Men took no offense at the mean estate of the Babe and his parents, that we may also not be offended in the mean estate of our neighbor, but rather see Christ in him, since the Kingdom of Christ is to be found among the lowly and the despised in persecution, misery, and the holy cross. Those who seek Christ anywhere else find him not. The Wise Men discovered him not at Herod's court, not with high priests, not in the great city of Jerusalem, but in Bethlehem, in the stable, with lowly folk, with Mary and Joseph. In a word, they found him where one would have least expected.

"They presented unto him gifts; gold, and frankincense, and myrrh."

Incense is a live confession, full of faith, by which we offer all that we have and are to God. The Wise Men traversed a long distance to bring this gift. Spiritually we can bring it swiftly and easily. The gift of our gold is that we should confess Christ as

King, laying aside our own esteem and the dictates of our reason and good intentions, that we should present ourselves as foolish, naked, and ready to be ruled. The sons of obedience are tractable, gladly accept their King, and bring all into submission to Christ. The incorrigibles who resist their King fall into tumult, anger, dissension, murmuring, and blasphemy. Thus we see that incense is faith and gold is hope, because faith believes that all things are and ought to be of God, and hope accepts and sustains what faith believes. The myrrh is love. Faith takes us from ourselves, that we should refer everything to God with praise and gratitude. Hope fills us with the concerns of others, that we may endure all in patience without resentment. Love reduces us to that nothing which we were in the beginning, so that we desire neither goods nor anything outside of God, but simply that we should commit ourselves truly to his good pleasure. This is the way of the cross by which we come most speedily into life.

We can present our gifts in the same way as the Lord says: "Inasmuch as ye have done it unto one of the least of these my brethren, ye have done it unto me." He who gives of his goods to help the poor, to send children to school, to educate them in God's Word and other arts that we may have good ministers—he is giving to the baby Jesus. He was not only born to poor and needy but also, on account of Herod, had at once to flee the country. On the journey into Egypt the presents of the Wise Men must have come in very handy. So in our day we should not forget those who are suffering persecution.

FLIGHT INTO EGYPT

Albrecht Dürer (1471-1528)

The untethered ox of its own accord follows the Holy Family.

The heads of cherubim fill the clouds.

The luxuriant foliage attracts attention.

Presentation

THE HARMONIZATION OF Matthew and Luke is a problem. Luke says that Joseph and Mary returned to Nazareth. Matthew says that they went down into Egypt. In any case they must have remained in Jerusalem for six weeks for the circumcision because the law did not allow it earlier.

According to the custom of the Jews, Mary took the baby Jesus to the Temple after forty days to be presented to the priest. There an aged man named Simeon took "him up in his arms, and blessed God, and said, Lord, now lettest thou thy servant depart in peace, according to thy word: For mine eyes have seen thy salvation, which thou hast prepared before the face of all people; a light to lighten the Gentiles, and the glory of thy people Israel."

When Mary heard such things spoken first by the angels, then shepherds, and now by Simeon, she wondered greatly. Wonderful, indeed, it was that such lowly and despised folk as Joseph and Mary should be the parents of such a Child! If all this had been said of the son of a high priest or a prince, it would not have been so marvelous. And now Simeon took the Child in his arms and declared him to be a Saviour, a light to the Gentiles and the glory of Israel.

Mary truly wondered at such words. We must recall that she was human and did not know and understand everything. All that had happened was as incredible to her as to anyone else. Nevertheless, she believed, and so must we all.

I have said before that his name means "Wonderful." He is like a grain of mustard seed which, though small, becomes great. Even so, that which is despised of men is great before God. This teaches us not to despair when the world turns against us, nor to say that God has turned away his eyes. His wonders no reason can comprehend. Wonderful is it that in the midst of death is life, in the midst of folly there is wisdom. Let us, then, take heart. How wonderful that the Child of a poor abandoned maid should become the King of the world! It does not make sense. Wonder brings faith. He who does not believe cannot understand, know, or see. He who understands cannot but wonder.

"And Simeon blessed them, and said unto Mary his mother, Behold, this child is set for the fall and rising again of many in Israel; and for a sign which shall be spoken against; (Yea, a sword shall pierce through thy own soul also) that the thoughts of many hearts may be revealed."

You have heard the Gospel: how the holy man blessed the holy mother and predicted that her Son should be for the rising and falling of many in Israel, a sign to be spoken against, and that a sword shall pierce her own soul that the secrets of many hearts should be revealed. These words are written so that we should not despair when we see great crowds falling away from Christ. If it had not been foreseen, it would have been unbearable. Simeon spoke of the fall and the sword as if he were saying: "Dear Mary, you have borne a Son. The world, the flesh, and the devil will be against him." What a congratulation this was to offer a mother of six weeks! He tells her that her Son is for a sign to be spoken against. First he blesses the Son, then speaks of his suffering and that all shall be against him. These words cut like a sword to Mary's heart. If all this had not been so clearly predicted throughout the prophets, no Christian could endure. Who can bear to see the Gospel so condemned, not to speak of the despite which rages among us? Why are men persecuted and killed for the sake of the Gospel? What has the little Child done? He announces: "My Father will be gracious to you and will free you from death, sin, and hell." And then men tread him underfoot and hang him on a cross as one accursed. Who can bear this? If I went by common sense, I would not be so patient as our Lord God when he offers men mercy and they curse him and pray to the devil.

God gives them this Child and he is to them a stone of stumbling and a sign of offense. The text relates that when Mary and Joseph brought Jesus into the Temple only two persons were there out of a populous city. Is it not shocking that from more then twenty thousand men only Simeon should be present? The priests pocketed the five groschen and paid no more attention to the Child. Is it not shameful? Ought not half the town at least have come out to see the Lord of all the world? But because there was no pomp, no one gave heed and Mary and Joseph brought him in alone. None but Simeon and Anna was there.

So it is today in the world, and even among Christians. The pope, the bishops, the fanatics, peasants, townsmen, nobles tread him underfoot, and I do it myself. I cannot believe in him as I should. He ought to be my true friend and comforter. But the "old donkey" in me won't have it, and the devil blows the bellows. In my heart it is just as bad as it is in the world. He is a sign to be spoken against.

Is not this a remarkable word that the fall should take place in Israel? If it were in Moab, Asia, Egypt, or Rome, it would not be so bad. But among the very people to whom the Child is given, the fall is to occur. Those who have the Gospel, who are baptized, who are Christians, will revile the Man. "Oh yes," you say, "but we do not defile the churches and the altars." No, you do not, but baptism, the teachings of Christ, and his innocent ministers are trampled upon and killed. This is destroying the very temple of God himself.

I could never have believed there could be such evil in the heart of man as I find now among peasants, townsmen, and nobles. I risked my life and never dreamed of this. I thought: "I will preach to them the true way, that they may be free. They will take it to heart." Had I known their hearts, a hundred horses could not have dragged me to it. I have often been sorry that I ever started to preach, but that is not right. As long as we live, we will preach to the honor of Christ and the comfort of the faithful, and let the world dance for gold and goods. Go on, my dear world, swagger while I laugh at you. We will see who comes off the better. For you this is the sign of a falling but for me of a rising. The secrets of your heart shall be revealed. This comfort the Gospel gives me.

The Magi came and went during the forty days before the presentation. Foiled by them, Herod resolved to destroy the Babe and worked on the supposition that he would still be in Bethlehem. To be sure of catching him, he killed all the children under two years. Such acts of bloodshed were not new to Herod. For three years he had been decimating the priests and nobles, especially in the Sanhedrin. He had two sons by a beloved wife, and yet executed both them and her, so that the Emperor Augustus said that he would rather be Herod's sow than his son. Yet the people did not rebel because they wanted a king of the seed of David and not a foreigner. When, then, the word came that such a king had been born, Herod was terror-stricken. "This bodes no good," thought he, and he called the Magi and told them to seek out the young Child so that he also might worship him. When he was mocked by them, he sad, "I will get him yet." All the children under two years were to be killed, not only in Bethlehem, but in the region round about. The time was set.

The slaughter by Herod of all the children of Bethlehem and the region about was a piece of sheer barbarism, but doubt not that Herod would find a plausible defense so that people would regard it, not as tyranny, but as necessary severity. The world is master of this art, when it goes against the Christians. Did not Christ say, "The time cometh, that whosoever killeth you will think that he doeth God service"? When the son of this Herod, named Herod Antipas, executed John the Baptist, he justified himself on the ground that he was an honorable man who could not go back on his word. When Christ was crucified and Stephen stoned, both were maligned as seditious and blasphemous. There are abundant examples in Scripture, and let no one doubt that Herod could devise a good case for the slaughter of the innocents. But how could he?

No doubt the priests gave him some good ideas, for we read that all Jerusalem was troubled with him. They would say: "If the word of this newborn king gets abroad, the Romans will be on our necks again. Then there will be bloodshed. So, dear Herod, if you have even a suspicion of where this child is, you had better do some strangling; otherwise our land will be wrecked."

Thus we see how the little baby Jesus, while still in the manger, filled the world with fear. Herod decided to cover the whole territory, lest the Child escape him. He could plausibly argue that it were better to bereave a few hundred fathers and mothers of their children than to ruin the whole land. The failure of the Wise Men to report only confirmed his suspicion that some plot was on foot. If the common people got wind of it, they might readily rise, whereas if they saw prompt action on the part of the government, they would be restrained. Thus Herod and his men took the sword, and became frightful murderers even though they put out such a persuasive defense that everyone thought they were keeping the peace.

Then the angel appeared at night to Joseph and said: "Fly! Up! Hurry! Fly!" He did not say, "Go"; he said, "Fly." Joseph awoke, and he did not think to himself: "There is no need to get started tonight. I will wait a couple of weeks, especially with a wife and child," but he said: "I cannot wait until daylight. Wake up, Mary, wake up! I am afraid your secret is out. Let's be gone, that those who seek us may not find. They had about twelve days' travel before leaving the territory of Herod. How should they find the way? What should they do? Joseph must have hurried in great concern, but he said to himself, "He who told me to go will lead me." He did not take time to put away anything in the house, but left everything.

What happened then to Christ happens now to the Gospel. But Herod failed. The angel warned Joseph in a dream, and God had already provided that the Wise Men should have made presents which well supplied the costs of the journey. Matthew says they gave gold, frankincense, and myrrh. It would have been a very considerable contribution, out of which Joseph and Mary could support themselves for some time, and perhaps the poor besides. The devil, Herod, and the priests meant to destroy Christ, but God provided the escape.

Before daylight the Holy Family were well beyond the Bethlehem town line. I doubt whether it was more than three miles from the village center.

The mothers in Bethlehem that evening fed porridge to their children, rocked the cradles, and went to sleep themselves without a care. The next morning there was not a household in Bethlehem in which there was not one child dead, or two or three. Then was there weeping because of this bloodhound, Rachel weeping for her children and refusing to be comforted. The children were taken straight to heaven as blessed martyrs, but what about the parents who would not be comforted? They did not understand that this was a spiritual testing because the Lord was come into the world in order that he might lay down his life.

Our little Lord we give thee praise;

Thou hast deigned to take our ways,

Born of a maid a man to be

And all the an-gels sing to Thee.

From Heaven High

Angel

From heaven high I come to earth. I bring you tidings of great mirth.
This mirth is such a wondrous thing that I must tell you all and sing.

A little child for you this morn has from a chosen maid been born,
A little child so tender, sweet, that you should skip upon your feet.

He is the Christ, our God indeed, who saves you all in every need.
He will himself your Saviour be. From all wrong doing make you free.

He brings you every one to bliss. The heavenly Father sees to this.
You shall be here with us on high. Here shall you live and never die.

Look now, you children, at the sign, a manger cradle far from fine.
A tiny baby you will see. Upholder of the world is he.

Children

How glad we'll be if it is so! With all the shepherds let us go
To see what God for us has done in sending us his own dear Son.

Look, look, my heart, and let me peek. Whom in the manger do
  you seek?

Who is that lovely little one? The Baby Jesus, God's own Son.
Be welcome, Lord; be now our guest. By you poor sinners have
     been blessed.
In nakedness and cold you lie. How can I thank you—how can I?

O Lord, who made and molded all, how did you come to be so small
That you should lie upon dry grass, the fodder of the ox and ass?

And if the world were twice as wide, with gold and precious
     jewels inside,
Still such a cradle would not do to hold a babe as great as you.

The velvet and the silken ruff, for these the hay is good enough.
Here lies a prince and Lord of all, a king within an ass's stall.

You wanted so to make me know that you had let all great things go.
You had a palace in the sky; you left it there for such as I.

O dear Lord Jesus, for your head now will I make the softest bed.
The chamber where this bed shall be is in my heart, inside of me.

I can play the whole day long. I'll dance and sing for you a song,
A soft and soothing lullaby, so sweet that you will never cry.

All

To God who sent his only Son be glory, laud, and honor done.
Let all the choir of heaven rejoice, the new ring in with heart
     and voice.